Conversations with Women CEO's & Leaders

The Confidence Factor for Women in Leadership

Conversations with Women CEOs & Leaders

Compiled by Carol Sankar

Conversations with Women CEO's & Leaders

The Confidence Factor for Women in Leadership

Conversations with Women CEOs & Leaders

Compiled by Carol Sankar

The Confidence Factor for Women in Leadership | Conversations with Women CEOs & Leaders Copyright © 2015 by Carol Sankar | The Confidence Factor for Women in Leadership

All rights reserved. No part of this book may be reproduced or transmitted in any form or by any means without written permission from the author.

ISBN 978-0-9833731-7-9
Printed by I.L. Press

Conversations With

Bev Vines-Haines & Charlotte Clary
 | *CEO's of Ice Chips Candy*

Cortney Baker
 | *CEO at KidsCare Therapy*

Helene Solomon
 | *CEO at Solomon McCown*

Patricia Baronowski-Schneider
 | *President of Prestine Advisors*

Adi Biran & Lihi Gerstner
 | *Co-Founders of Splacer*

Kristen Koh-Goldstein
 | *CEO Scalus*

Deborah Sweeney
 | *CEO of My Corporation*

Suzanne Garber
 | *CEO of Gauze*

Lori Cheek
 | *CEO of Cheek'd*

Rachel Maxwell

| CEO of Maxwell Biometrics

Sheila Talton
| CEO of Gray Matter Analytics

Paige Arnof-Fenn
| Founder & CEO Mavens & Moguls

Maria Ioia
| CEO of Market Intelligence Agency

Marne Martin
| CEO of Service Power Technologies

Carol Sankar
| Founder of RRC

Hedy Popson
| President of Productions Plus

Eileen McDonnell
| CEO of Penn Mutual Life

Lori Florio & Emily Vitale
| Founders of PRISMSPORT

Before we get started

These are the conversations I wished I had when I first started my company. The journey, the learning, the pitfalls, the lessons and the successes have all been worth it; but when I was seeking a high level woman to mentor me in the beginning, it seemed impossible.

As a woman, leadership can be a lonely place. When you have the desire to build something bigger than anyone else can imagine, then you feel the push of the "glass ceiling" and gender expectations baring down on you as you try to push your way to the top. As women, I believe that we need male mentors to help us build our confidence, but we also need women in leadership to show us how to balance the expectations.

I now realize that we can have it all. It took me almost 10 years to come to that realization. We can have everything we desire, but not at the same time. In my career, I have had to make some harsh personal choices that continue to impact my family. I had to give up the notion that there is a real "work/life balance" for high level women. My new method is do what are in my core strengths first, admit the things that I cannot do next, and delegate the things that will slow me down from my purpose last. Therefore, I cannot be super mom, super wife and super CEO at the same time.

Once you raise the bar around you and create categories for your gifts, the universe will reward you for being honest with yourself. Being a leader is tough, yet rewarding. Do not approach it unless you are ready for a high level of sacrifice and commitment.

The women in this compilation have achieved great success, while making sacrifices. I am honored that I experienced these conversations and I am grateful for their transparency to share their journey with you. I believe that women need to hear how high level women make the leap to extraordinary success. Welcome to Conversations with Women CEOs & Leaders.

Conversations with Women CEO's & Leaders

My Conversation With
Bev Vines-Haines & Charlotte Clary
CEO's of Ice Chips Candy

When we formulated Ice Chips candy, we were not intending to create a phenomenon and a million-dollar company. We were two grandmas hoping to make a safe and healthy treat for our total of forty-one grandchildren. At the time, we were already busy with a natural skin care company and had plenty of obligations at work and at home.

Nonetheless, Ice Chips candies was an instant hit and we quickly shifted our focus. Our confidence leaped when friends, families and even stores begged for more candy and more flavors. In less than five years, Ice Chips became a multi-million dollar business. Growth, while exciting, comes with lots of growing pains. The first batches of Ice Chips were made in a single car garage that had been converted into a kitchen. Then, there was a brand new two car garage. From there we moved to a 4500 square foot facility and eventually added space there. But continued growth demanded even more space and today nearly fifty employees make, package, sell and ship this amazing candy from a 21,500 square foot plant.

In 2012 Bev and I appeared on ABC's hit show, Shark Tank. That was the catalyst that took us from being a west coast wonder to a nationwide sensation. Once we appeared on the show and the Sharks referred to us as *the Grannies*, people all over the country felt comfortable calling us Grannie Bev and Grannie Charlotte. Obviously with all the growth and sales, we needed to increase production. While in our last shop, we could produce 9500 tins of candy each day, we can now produce 50,000 units (both the familiar tins and a new pouch size) daily.

Selling to box stores and large chain businesses is more involved and time consuming than selling to small chains and individual health food stores. Ice Chips had to adjust to that new form of sale while still catering to the small businesses that brought our first success. It takes a delicate balance and a willingness to absorb new lessons in order to manage employees, keep up with countless government forms, acquire and run automation machinery, and still participate in marketing, social media and obtaining new customers.

Greater sales demand greater understanding of sound business practices. Obstacles have included rapid growth, a couple "copy cat" products where imitators plagiarized nutrition content and virtually every word on Ice Chip packaging. It is complicated to lead a business through the maze required for success.

The proudest achievement would have to be the fact we possessed the courage demanded to take a good idea and develop it into a multi-million dollar reality. That would not be easy for young business graduates fresh out of school. At a certain age it is easier to sit down and live off memories and former successes. Bev and I cast off easy and went for tough: risking everything in a challenged economy, at an age when many people quit. Instead we pressed on for the impossible.

These days, we enjoy a national sales force, an Operations Manager, a Financial Adviser as well as attorneys, a CPA and all the other experts needed when a business explodes. Many families enjoy an Ice Chips' life. We delight in watching our employees grow with the company and develop careers none of them could imagine just five years ago.

Conversations with Women CEO's & Leaders

My Conversation With

Cortney Baker, M.S., CCC/SLP
CEO/Owner, KidsCare Therapy and Baker Management Group

I think I officially began my adult journey when I was 12. My only sibling, my sister who was 4 years older than I, was diagnosed with Multiple Sclerosis and I watched her deteriorate quickly right in front of my eyes. She had such a progressive form of the disease that, at 18, she had difficulty walking, talking, feeding, and bathing herself. Because our parents were divorced and we were shuffled back and forth between visitation schedules, we were each other's constants. Kim's doctors had told us that by her 21st birthday that she would either be bedridden or in a wheelchair for life. I helped take care of her on her journey until she died suddenly of a heart defect when she was 20. It was one month after my 16th birthday.

At 18 I found myself in a broken relationship with a baby on the way. I got pregnant; he left. My father, who had raised me up until that point, told me that if I was going to keep the baby that I couldn't raise the child at his house. I had an adoptive family picked out for my son, but once I felt him move in my womb I knew that I couldn't go through with the adoption. I moved in with my mom and her new husband and continued in my double-shift job of waiting tables to make ends meet. I turned 19 in September and got a rocking chair for my birthday. I had my son, Landon, two months later.

Fast forward through a few years and a failed marriage and a move out of state where I knew no one. I had my son, who quickly became my closest companion, and enrolled in junior college and then began attending the local university, where I completed my Master's degree in communication disorders and sciences in 2001.

In 2003, at the age of 28, with a brand new marriage and a new baby on the way, I started my own pediatric home healthcare agency in Dallas as the solo therapist with 10 patients who were willing to take a chance on me. Today KidsCare Therapy is operational throughout the state of Texas and have the blessing of providing services to over 1700 patients and help support nearly 300 employees.

Life hasn't been easy. In fact, so far from it. I have suffered from lack of self-confidence in my abilities and decisions, both personally and professionally. In 2012, at the age of 37, I suffered a stroke in two places while at home. That was in September and then in January 2013 I started in the doctoral program for Organizational Leadership at Pepperdine University.

To identify my proudest moment to this point, I think that's hard to say. I was so proud at my wedding, to know that I was marrying my best friend and the love of my life. I was also so proud when I had both of my daughters, too. And then I was such a proud mom when my son graduated from high school and was accepted to the University of Texas at Austin, a difficult school to get into as an incoming freshman. I think overall, personally, though, was when I was conducting my research for my dissertation, entitled Women Leaders in Healthcare: Going Beyond the Glass Ceiling. I met some incredible women who really opened their hearts and lives to me to explain what challenges they had been on in their journey. So many of them described how their confidence had held them back. All I could say was, "ME TOO!"

The one thing I can speak to about my confidence, though, is that I am where I am because I never gave up. I have had adversity, as we all do, from the time I was 4 and my parents divorced. I also have such an immense faith that has seen me through so many of the darkest days of my life, especially when dealing with my sister's death and a failed first marriage. Without my faith and belief in the fact that I am a child of God, I would have probably folded a long time ago. Even after I had my stroke, after achieving greater success than I could ever imagine, I suffered a horrible depression. I was worried about ever being able to be whole and well again. But by the grace of God, I am 99% restored. So thankful for everyday miracles that happen to ordinary people like me.

Last year I was honored to be one of the top 3 Texas Business Women of the Year. What an honor and accomplishment for a single mom who had no direction other than waiting tables.

Conversations with Women CEO's & Leaders

My Conversation With
Helene Solomon
Founder & CEO of Solomon McCown

I was always a shy person growing up in New York City, in high school and even through my college years at Boston University, I was much more reserved than many of my friends and classmates.

All of that changed when I entered politics in 1978, landing a job for former Boston Mayor Kevin White, and became active in his political organization, where I was given a list of 30 residents who were considered "super voters" in my Allston-Brighton neighborhood.

My job was to build a personal relationship with each of them, ensuring that when it came time for the election, they would vote for Kevin White.

To my surprise, I soon found that I enjoyed knocking on my neighbors' doors, talking and getting to know each one, and building a rapport with them. I realized that this was an opportunity for me to help build a stronger link between the neighborhood where I lived and the city of Boston.

Many of the older voters would invite me into their homes and tell me about their lives and history living in the neighborhood. I found each voter's story quite interesting, and learned a valuable business and life lesson from that experience. If you listen to people, you have a better understanding of how to relate to them. This was the point in my life where I started to gain my confidence because I learned how to read people, and from there, I could try and help them.

I was 25 years old.

Fast forward five years. At 30, after meeting many of my neighbors and networking with those in local political circles, I decided to run for City Council. My co-workers from City Hall and my friends all encouraged me because of the relationships I had built over time working politically in my neighborhood.

I narrowly lost in a very tight election, but running for office helped me gain even more confidence. Public debates, knocking on more doors, meeting and greeting people on street corners all over the city and being in the public limelight and constantly in local media, my shyness as a child and young adult faded quickly. I realized that I enjoyed and wanted to help people. I wanted to be around people, listen to their issues and try hard to help solve them.

So I decided to start a consulting business. I wanted to take all of my ideas and marry them to the relationships with those who I could relate to on a personal level. I used all the connections I made under Kevin White and the City to package my skills and offer them as services.

I started with issues that were important to me, such as affordable housing and rent control. At the time, the largest condo conversion on the east coast was taking place at the Brook House in Brookline. Once more, I found myself going door-to-door, talking to elderly tenants and letting them know they had nothing to fear and would not be evicted.

This instilled quite a bit of confidence in me because I was exposed to high-powered real estate developers, making sure the issue was understood at all levels and assuring town meeting members, tenants and their relatives that their homes were still their homes and they would not be affected by the conversion.

I had my consulting business for three years before I founded my first PR agency. This was a great learning experience and a good confidence builder as I spent most of my time networking, talking to people working in various industries and raising my profile.

Then, when my partner, Ashley McCown, and I founded our current PR agency, Solomon McCown & Company in 2003, we knew the type of business we wanted to build.

There were a few economic downturns that tested our resolve, but we maintained our confidence knowing that we were providing services in a consistently different way than our competitors. Over the last five years growing the agency, our confidence has increased dramatically. We know who we are, our positions in the industry and we have the self-assurance to say no to prospects, fire clients who aren't the right fit for our firm, and we are able to be more selective enabling us to provide laser-focused attention to relationships we want to keep for a long time.

One of our well-known practice areas is crisis communications, where we are called upon to provide damage control or planning. During these delicate times, you need to have total confidence in the strategic counsel you are offering – there is no margin for error. But the ability to be candid with those involved and build their trust has consistently helped raise our confidence.

One of the obstacles I've recently been able to overcome, and one that I've struggled with since starting our business, is having the confidence to let go of certain responsibilities and trust in my capable employees to handle that workload. The most important part of my job as CEO is hiring the people who I believe in and can trust. I would say that my greatest achievement is seeing those same employees develop. I love watching my staff grow as professionals and having the confidence to let them try new things and spread their wings.

I've come a long way since those shy days as a young. In the last two years, we've reached some major milestones, including opening a New York office, creating a digital division and video department, working with the influential leaders and CEOs of the sectors we focus in, and winning 79 industry awards over our 12-year run. 2015 is going to be another banner year for us as we continue to hit all of these benchmarks of growth. I believe that our confidence and success since starting the agency will only continue to escalate in the years to come, and I look forward to enjoying this wonderful ride.

Conversations with Women CEO's & Leaders

My Conversation With
Patricia Baronowski-Schneider
President, Pristine Advisers

I can thank the institutions at the tip of lower Manhattan for giving me my confidence because, if the pavement at the corner of Wall and Broad Street is more tarred than golden, if cynicism is the coin of the realm and cronyism is the currency of power, there is still the transmission of light; rays that seep through the cracks to tell us the story of our country, like the beams that travel the heavens to reveal the birth of our universe, so we may move forward with knowledge and wisdom.

Thinking I could work on Wall Street – believing I *would* work on Wall Street – is all the confidence one can want.

Confidence is essential to overcoming various challenges, which, with regard to the obstacles that define the early years of my career, involve attracting clients for my financial communications and investor relations firm.

From these events, I found my confidence in - and continue to renew my confidence, by working with managers of Fortune 500 Companies, as well as managers of financial firms and closed-end investment funds, who know that impressive returns on investments will fail to impress industry analysts (and fail to impress prospective clients) without the ability to communicate effectively.

Meeting with these managers, who tend to have a greater fluency with numbers than words, that their command of the vernacular of everyday speech does not match their mastery of mathematics and finance, I must explain to them why my services are valuable; I must prove how, together, we can convert complex data into intelligible ideas and actionable intelligence; that numbers can be numbing, and that these figures exist in a vacuum, without a story that makes a firm or fund's performance worth hearing.

By demonstrating that words have meaning, that people invest their confidence in the power and accuracy of words, I help professionals– the very people who once challenged the value of my services– to give potential investors the confidence they need to make an informed decision about where to invest their respective funds.

I am grateful for having faced these tests, which does not mean I want to face them again . . . because I do not. But those things, amplified by the risks of entering new territories and coarsened by the pessimism and pretension of others, are the reason why I am a confident professional and the head of a my own business.

I am also a licensed skydiver. I was terrified of heights and took a leap of faith to get over that fear – and thus, my passion for skydiving began 15 years ago. 3000 jumps' later, skydiving has given me more confidence than one could ask for. When you can take a leap from 13.5k feet in the air every weekend, it is hard to rattle me. I have conquered my fears and am confident in all that I do.

I look back at the image in my mind, so I can hear the coda to my initial remarks of self-doubt. The words echo with their sounds of optimism and security:
"Do not stop. Do not surrender. I will only yield when every opportunity is gone, when every chance to network is over and when the will is no

more. Until then, I must live – gloriously, proudly, unapologetically and, yes, confidently."

That statement is a personal oath. It is boastful, in part, but it is never arrogant because it is so real.

I have too many injuries – I bear too many badges from the battlefield, so to speak – to think I am supreme.

Life teaches me that confidence is an asset, while arrogance, with all its bravado and ignorance – with all its narcissism and vanity – is full of courageous talk and cowardly behavior.

A leader is confident because she must be. Confidence helps us to stand tall, take risks, think outside the box, be different, and above all – never settle for less than you deserve. Between my leap of faith 15 years and 3000 jumps ago, to my battlegrounds in the workforce, I have grown by leaps and bounds in the confidence department. The old adage, "that which does not break you only makes you stronger" is my credo.

My Conversation With
Adi Biran & Lihi Gerstner
co-founder and CPO at Splacer

Throughout our careers as architects, lecturers, and researchers, we identified a striking contrast between the limited amount of urban infrastructures, the consequent soaring prices of real estate and cost of living, and the fact that so many wonderful spaces remain empty and underutilized for many hours. This seemingly reverse correlation was the start of our journey, which led us to co-found Splacer together.

In a world where access governs ownership, the platform we created allows people to list, discover and explore spaces for event experiences, based on short-term bookings. Since space is the most expensive asset, our working hypothesis is based on the premise that the way people use properties can be made more efficient. Spaces can be utilized in a variety of innovative ways, by a variety of people, and they can embody values of sustainability, collaboration, experimentation and inspiration if we simply change how we perceive, share and communicate them. In that regard, Splacer is invested in planning sustainable cities, and the pursuit of inspiring aesthetics. We see through the details; we recognize the added value of a given space; and, we know people create better in an interesting environment.

As two professional women, collaborating and working together, we have come to experiences on our path differently, and we help one another to feel more confident along the way. Our partnership is a key aspect of our strength as individuals and our ability to push our organization forward. We discovered our confidence not through a singular event, but over time, by not giving up on creating the system we truly believed is necessary, and realizing people began using Splacer and sharing spaces in our hometown and beta site - Tel Aviv. We established connections with companies such as Facebook, Fiverr, and Outbrain, and located potential creative spaces for corporate and private events. Whereas the time spent developing Splacer as a product was of experimentation and investigation, the reactions we received after sharing it with the world validated our observations, analysis and working model. This confidence prepared us for the high and low moments we encountered since then.

Being women venturing as first timers into the world of startup business, we knew we were about to get rejected often. Like so many other entrepreneurs, we experienced failure on a daily basis. However, you cannot embark on such a project without being ready for refusals and dismissals. Since the field of technology and startups was foreign to us, we knew we were about to make many mistakes. When you realize, however, you only have a 2% chance to succeed, failure seems inevitable and this thought drove us forward -- you work hard and embrace the potential to fail, and amazingly, this becomes an engine that drives innovation and growth. We felt that more strongly since we embarked on this project together than we did throughout our entire careers. And indeed, by July 1, 2015, we were able to announce we raised $1.4 million in seed funding. We also had offices in Tel Aviv and New York and close to 200 listings on our website. The "splace" owners became part of this growing community: they were now our partners in a series of events and curated collaborations. Crucially, we found ourselves contributing to and transforming the parameters of the conversation we recognized and had initially set out to articulate.

My Conversation With
Kristen Koh-Goldstein
CEO of Scalus

Three Tips for Upping Your Confidence Factor

I found my confidence factor when I realized my politeness came at the cost of authenticity, which made me less effective. My experience ranges over two hugely different sectors--global financial institutions and lean startups--and contrasting the way I functioned in each of them informed my confidence factor.

Say what you mean in the open, rather than behind closed doors.

In an innovative and fast-moving environment, consensus building (what was considered polite in the financial institutions I worked at) looks like politicking. When I came to my first startup, I saw my colleagues own the room by leading any given proposal with the punchline and then letting the team poke holes in it, rather than lead up to a recommendation with evidence. They did not politick or build consensus prior to speaking their minds at executive team meetings--they didn't have time for that. As a result, decisions were made faster and the company embraced change. As I internalized and delivered this style, I noticed that I did not get interrupted as often as when I took time to build my case.

Recognize and bridge different collaboration styles.

I founded my third company Scalus because as the founder of BackOps, I realized the disconnect between the collaboration style between my staff and clients was causing the service delivery failures rather than the actual work product. Clients did not respond well to the case building my accounting staff was conditioned to do. Clients frequently ignored my staff because of the inability to discern signal from noise - what information did my client really need. They responded better to me, who would lead with "you need to pay your bills now or the lights go out and everyone goes home," rather than the illustration of that point from our accountants at the next level of detail.

Scalus is designed to meet the needs of meticulous and detail-oriented people, many of whom are in compliance ridden industries, to run business processes with consistency and keep order. It also meets the needs of those who prefer the table of contents over the details of the books--it gives a high level overview of what's flowing and what's taking too long, and makes it obvious what's about to fall off of the table. Neither style is better, you need both in any organization, but you must recognize the differences and take advantage of them to be successful.

Teach through example - live it every day.

I have been the beneficiary of some of the best mentoring and learning available, and I believe it's important to pay that forward -- especially as I see collaboration clashes play out again and again. To any mentee or new staff member, I recommend three habits:

- *Speak your mind with immediacy and directness*, because authenticity fosters trust and gets things done quickly.
- *Do not edit reality.* When you sugar-coat or phase bad news, you are degrading the team's ability to make good decisions.
- *Stop apologizing* for conditions not in your direct control. If you apologize for the

weather or for faulty office equipment, you are being careless with blame.

Of course, nobody is perfect. No one is totally immune to gender conditioning. But I have found that as my team members and mentees are able to break through these habits, they are also more conscious with their words and actions in the collaboration context and they settle into a confidence factor themselves.

My Conversation With

Deborah Sweeney
CEO of My Corporation

I found my confidence factor when I realized that I could be who I am in business without having to fit a particular mold. When I started practicing law, I had a drive to develop my own business – to be a rain maker and contributor in my law firm. I didn't want to be the traditional 'associate' doing very basic work.

I had a drive to develop and grow business and I knew I wanted to focus in the area of intellectual property law. I was able to develop contacts and build a strong network of business. It was my goal to become partner before having children. In fact, my husband, also an attorney, always suggested that we wait to have kids until I attained partnership status. We both knew that there would obstacles in the law firm world once we had children.

After having my first son, I was fortunate enough to be offered an in-house position at one of my clients, MyCorporation.com. After six months, we negotiated a deal to sell the company to Intuit. After a few years, I was appointed to run the division. I really gained confidence working in a corporate role with both a legal and business background. It was a fantastic opportunity, but it was corporate! I was traveling and in meetings full time. I was pregnant with my second son and an opportunity presented itself where I offered to buy the business out of Intuit and take MyCorporation private. I presented to the leadership team at Intuit and subsequently purchased MyCorporation out.

I realized throughout these opportunities and changes that you should always take opportunities and seize them. Confidence is critical. I knew that if I went into each situation with confidence and a sense of ability to thrive in each situation, I would find success. My confidence in business allowed me to take risks that I might not otherwise have taken. I knew that I could potentially not have attained my goals – making partner, going in-house, helping to get the business acquired by Intuit, purchasing the business out of Intuit and then turning the business around to profitability and sustained growth.

Confidence in myself and my abilities made the difference. I knew that owning a business and turning it to a profitable growing venture would be a daunting task, but I also knew I was up for the challenge. This was the opportunity of a lifetime.

Now, I have the benefit of being the master of my own destiny. I work a lot, but I work on my own schedule. I spend time with my sons and family and I recognize the importance of balance. I, however, love to work! I love that I can be creative and innovative. I love that I can employ fantastic people and learn from them. I love that owning this business makes me a better parent, a more well-rounded person, and even more confident. I did not decide to follow the traditional path of law and practice in a law firm despite the long hours, and often less family-friendly environment. I decided to forge my own path – to take opportunities as they presented themselves and many times, to create opportunities myself!

Each time I did this, I felt more reassured in my desire to be who I wanted to be – to prioritize both family and career and to make the best of it. I have enjoyed every step of the way and I think my confidence has enabled me to do that. My confidence also flows to my children – they feel proud of their mom who has given it all and they know the pride I take in what I have created!

My Conversation With
Suzanne Garber
CEO of Gauze

I am CEO of Gauze, a healthcare technology firm that connects patients with international hospitals. Prior to Gauze, I was the COO of a $1.5Bn international medical assistance firm and the Managing Director of a $35Bn logistics enterprise based in Brazil. My trajectory has been pretty meteoric, thanks to the help of expert mentors, and here's what I've learned along the way:

1) Find a mentor. Some advocate against mentors in the traditional sense and some are for formalized relationships. Whatever or however you choose to engage another individual with more experience, wisdom and maturity than you--DO IT. You cannot solve every problem on your own and you will be surrounded by many 'yes' people who won't tell you the truth; you need to find someone who will tell you the ugly truth of when you've made a dog of a decision or that you're not as stupid as the critics are saying.

2) Take calculated risks. Oftentimes, people think that unless they are continually receiving promotions, they are not advancing in their career. In fact, many see lateral moves as

demotions when nothing could be farther than the truth if done strategically. This means taking calculated risks such as taking a position in a different department (particularly one that is male-dominated like supply chain or operations) or even moving offshore. With each move and different environment (physical or professional) you will learn new things you would never have had the opportunity to experience had you stayed in your comfy, cushy previous position. And, you'll gain confidence along the way knowing you've just blown your own expectation out of the water!

3) Build your safety network. In my book, "SAFETY NETwork: A Tale of Ten Truths of Executive Networking" I interviewed 100+ C-level executives on how they could have avoided the inevitable pitfalls that besiege even the most distinguished of careers. Building their network outside of their own companies was number one. I see that in my life as well and I'm continually amazed at the opportunities that organically present themselves to me simply because I had the spunk and audacity to reach out to others beyond corporate walls and geographic

boundaries. Building your network also helps you broaden your own knowledge by interacting with others with different (or stronger) skill sets than yourself. Remember, iron sharpens iron.

My Conversation With

Lori Cheek
CEO of Cheek'd

Coming from a career of making nearly $120K a year, living a pretty fabulous life traveling, dining out and shopping like it was my job in one of the most expensive cities in the world, I came up with an idea that I had to bring to life... In May of 2010, I launched Cheekd.com —a mobile app that makes "missed connections" obsolete. After finishing off my savings from my 15 year career in architecture, I had to get extremely creative to continue funding my business and this is where the financial sacrifices began... I made nearly $75,000 by selling my designer clothes at consignment shops and on eBay, doing focus groups, secret shopping and by selling my electronics and other odds and ends around my apartment on Craigslist that all went straight back into my business. The biggest chunk of cash came from renting out my West Village Studio in NYC on AirBnB, while I couch surfed for 14 months, nearly got evicted and ultimately lost my lease of 5 years in my gorgeous apartment.

And the journey started here::::

Seven years ago, I was out to dinner with a friend & architectural colleague and I had excused myself from the table. When I returned, my handsome friend had scribbled on the back of his business card, "want to have dinner?" As we were leaving the restaurant, he slid that card to an attractive woman at a nearby table. He left with a pending date. I left with an idea... It had happened to me a thousand times during my NYC commute—spotting that intriguing stranger on a train, in a café, crossing the street, at baggage claim, etc. and nearly 999 of them got away. Handing a business card could have been one answer, but I was entranced by the mysterious gesture of handing it to the object of your affection and removing the personal details included on a typical business card, which is simply too much information to hand to a total stranger. A person's name on a card, alone, could potentially lead you to their front door.

My solution to the problem would apply a personal approach to online dating by moving the initial encounter offline with a smooth physical introduction. The Saturday afternoon after coming up with the idea of Cheek'd, I gathered a group of friends at the Soho House, added many bottles of wine and we spent the day brainstorming about lines, designs and ideas for the (soon to be named) "Cheek'd" cards. I continued this concept and branding process for a few months while working my full time job at Vitra, the Swiss/ German furniture/ design company. I'd never started my own business and struggled with the actual "business" side of creating the company. I found myself walking around in circles with this great idea for almost a year until I was introduced to my now Co-Founder at a party, who suggested we sit down the following Monday morning and bring the idea to life. We met, as suggested, and by the end of the week had a Business Plan and started the process of incorporating, patenting, trademarking, sourcing vendors, building the site, etc. Nearly one year after my initial meeting with him, we launched in May of 2010. A few months later, we popped up on the cover of the Styles Section of The New York Times... "Move over, Match.com, this is the next generation of online dating." A couple of days later, I got a call from Oprah Winfrey's Studio asking for an interview. I knew I had gold in my hands. I left my job and started working full time on Cheekd in November of 2010 and soon after, Cheek'd went global with customers in 47 states in America and 28 countries internationally but that didn't make for instant success....

And finally, after four tumultuous years of building my startup with the wrong partners, lots of bad decisions and some major rookie mistakes, I was determined to find a way to take my business to the next level ... and what better way than to apply to ABC's Shark Tank. In September of 2013, I found myself walking down that scary shark infested hallway into a stare off with 5 of the harshest millionaire investors in the world. I'd never been more nervous in my entire life. When I proclaimed I was going to change the population with my reverse engineered online dating business, serial entrepreneur and Dallas Mavericks owner, Mark Cuban, rolled his eyes, called me delusional and immediately snapped, "I'm out." Billionaire investor, Kevin O'Leary, demanded that I quit my "hobby" and shoot my business—my passion– like a rabid dog. After getting shot down by all five Sharks, I looked them in the eye and said, "Trust that you'll all see me again."

Although those final bold words of mine ended up on the cutting room floor (adding insult to injury), in the 48 hours after the broadcast, Cheekd.com received a record breaking 100K unique visitors and our inbox filled up with thousands of emails insisting that the "Sharks" were "out of their minds" for not investing. A little under 50 of those emails were from interested investors. Since the Shark Tank aired in February of this year, I found the missing link from years before. I've gotten a CTO on board who's helped facilitate and finance the new face and technology behind the new Cheekd. The newly launched dating app allows users to solve missed connections with a new technology that was not available when the patented Cheekd idea was launched in 2010. It was only a matter of time and I'm thankful I didn't take the Sharks advice to quit and move on.

While the physical cards worked anywhere in the world and were a perfect way to break the ice, we found a few barriers; the main one being that our users were still quite intimidated to walk up and slip a card to a total stranger. Looking into alternatives of ways we could change the platform, we discovered a way to make these IRL encounters much easier and less intimidating via a mobile solution.

Previously, with the Cheek'd Version1, users would use a set of clever cards to introduce themselves to individuals they encounter in the offline world who sparked their interest. If the interest was mutual, the card recipients used the card's unique code to reconnect easily with the person via a private online profile viewable at Cheekd.com.

The newly launched Cheekd reimagines online dating with a new app that makes missed connections obsolete. Cheekd uses a cross-platform low energy Bluetooth technology, which fosters hyper local engagement. The app connects people in real time, versus virtual time. Connections begin in person; Cheekd helps you take the next step and continue the conversation online.

Cheekd ensures you 'Never Miss a Connection'; thanks to this new Bluetooth technology, the app works on the train; on a plane... anywhere—You'll get a notification if someone who meets your criteria is within 30 feet of you. If you're near a potential spark, Cheekd makes sure you know about it.

Cheekd has been the most powerful thing that's ever happened to me. Building this business has been an incredible learning experience. I've taken a major risk (both financially & mentally) and surrendered my career in architecture & design, but my heart and mind are in this project every waking moment. I've never been more dedicated to anything. Despite the occasional overwhelming stress, it's been loads of fun. I feel like I'm living the American Dream—I've given birth to an invention. I've gone from 15 years of helping others build their dreams to a life finally dedicated to building my own. It's the most rewarding feeling. I'm at a ramp right now and I'm ready to fly! Our newly launched app has been awarded the Mobile Week 2015 NYC Champions as well as the Data of Love 2.0 Pitch event over the past few weeks.

Conversations with Women CEO's & Leaders

My Conversation With
Rachel Maxwell
CEO of Maxwell Biometrics, INC

I found my confidence when I realized that all I whatever need was God.

God was all I had. There was a small church I used to go to out in Pasadena, CA. I had gone through an incredibly dark time in my life, and I'd go and pray there on my way to school.

What I went through was no small feat- lets just say it was an incredibly violent event and he pled guilty.

But in the process I began to realize who I truly was, and I lost a great deal of people who I thought were friends.

The final straw came from a friend of mine who had been a source of strength, a shoulder to lean on- in this time of great darkness he suggested we have an affair. He wanted to "teach me" what he had "taught" his wife.

I ran away as fast as I could- and there I was, alone.

I went back to that little church – and I began to pray incessantly. I was angry, confused, and in state of agony. We'll call it despair.

I asked God for someone- just one good soul to talk to, to lean on- and I couldn't understand the point of this isolation.

Out of nowhere a man came from behind the altar, he saw me came to my pew and hugged me. I tried to explain my situation through my tears, and I was RELIEVED that God had answered my prayers.

The man- who was a bit bigger, began to explain to me that we all have problems, and that at times he ate too much... Well I'll paraphrase what he said...

"You know we all have problems, I'm sad because I eat too much and I eat too much because I'm sad- it's like kids who play in gardens and ruin your flowers."

I remember looking up at the altar... Puzzled. Here I explain the darkest most disturbing experience of my life – one that landed me in the hospital- and he was talking about his eating problems, food and kids wrecking gardens. Now I'm not saying that one struggle is greater or lesser than the other; but I still remember looking up at the alter somewhat confused; I began to see why the isolation had happened in the first place. I remember smiling, almost laughing at God's beautiful humor. I felt this wonderful presence of God and, that day, I realized no matter what happens I would always have God- and in reality that's all you ever need in this world. If you have God you have everything – and nothing or no one has power to rule your life. You can change and affect the world in so many ways, and it's all possible with faith. Faith in yourself, though your faith in God. Doesn't matter if you're a Mom, Teacher, Professor, Driver, Scientist or head of a corporation; in this life, it's you and God, and when you realize that, your life becomes limitless.

"If God is for us, who can be against us?"

Conversations with Women CEO's & Leaders

My Conversation With
Sheila Talton
President & CEO at Gray Matter Analytics

The tech industry is continuously criticized for the lack of women in leadership roles. According to US Bureau of Labor Statistics, women hold 47% of all jobs, but just 25.6% of computer and mathematical occupations. There is a vast shortage of women in big data analytics, but a surfeit of qualified women that are up for the job.

A Need for Diversity in the Workplace
Diversity is a crucial component within any business, as company leaders tend to get more out of their employees when all ages, genders and nationalities work together. Diversity in a tech company or startup is pertinent for innovation. For example, when it comes to gender, men and women are wired differently and bring different viewpoints and ideas to the table, which results in more efficient problem-solving for companies. Women who are prepared and work hard have the collaborative skills, presentation skills, and sense of usability that are all crucial in the tech world. Fortunately, tech is an industry wherein the talented are chosen and moved ahead on the basis of their achievements. That being the case, women have the opportunity to be selected for

these leadership roles on the basis of intellectual criteria; it's simply a matter of getting women into the field in the first place.

Breaking into the Tech Industry

According to the ESA, women hold a disproportionately low share of STEM undergraduate degrees, particularly in engineering, and women with a STEM degree are less likely than their male counterparts to work in a STEM occupation. The lack of women in leadership roles within the industry starts with the dearth of opportunities for women to actively engage in data science courses. The thought of jumping into a male-dominated field can be very intimidating for women unless they have experience and confidence, which early schooling can provide. If girls in high school are given the option to study computer science, and women in college then take the requisite engineering courses, upon graduation they will have the necessary schooling and experience to begin their careers and remain in these fields long-term. Thankfully, most universities are now offering advanced analytics classes, which women can take advantage of to indoctrinate them into the data analytics arena. That being said, once women get into the industry, it is important to stay in the industry. The retention rate plays a large role in determining whether or not these women can be considered for leadership positions within the industry.

The ease at which women can overcome these gender gaps depends upon where women are at in their career. If it is at the onset, they should familiarize themselves with the applications of whatever type of technology they are working with. A student can take graduate-level classes without getting an actual graduate degree and train to become a data or business analyst instead. If they are not software engineers, mathematicians or statisticians, women can consider positions in sales, marketing, customer interfacing or customer support, which offer them a foot in the door without needing an advanced technology degree right from the start. There are numerous roles within business and data analytics that may not be leadership roles, but are still imperative for a successful company to remain strong. For women who are mid-career or more senior-level, they can focus on the support roles for major technology firms in marketing, sales, human resources, legal, financing, or customer service.

Hiring Women Where it's Needed.
Because women don't already have a strong presence within the tech field, they often aren't considered for stretch roles. According to American Association of University Women, only 26 percent of computing jobs in the U.S. were held by women. Company leaders will often consider men for these positions even if they don't necessarily have the complete background because they have historically only seen men's success here. If there were more senior women within these companies, there would be more opportunity for women to get a shot at a role that perhaps they haven't done before.

There are many industries that are female-friendly, such as healthcare and retail. Companies that are operating predominantly in those industries should make it a high priority to engage women. Women can be involved in the companies that are building the data analytics, software development or building algorithms in those particulars.

Arguably the greatest advantage to operating in a tech career is the fact that it is a growth industry. This allows anyone to begin at the bottom and maintain longevity in the field. I have been operating in this industry for 30 years, and even when you have a down turn, people that have great skills can always reinvigorate their career as long as they are knowledgeable and competent. A growth industry affords you the ability be a mature company as well as startup company and you can even float throughout your career. The advantages and opportunities for women in tech are endless if they are willing to make the shift forward.

The tech industry as of now is male-dominated, but the shift can happen if companies begin implementing the recruitment of women as part of performance evaluations more often, giving these women a fair opportunity. Women must be judged on their ability to perform and be seen as engineers, data scientists, mathematicians and designers. We are not "women engineers"; we are engineers. We are not "women data analysts"; we are data analysts. We are equal in capability, but diverse in merit, and as long as women believe that, they can enter the tech workforce confidently and help begin the process of slowly closing this decades-long gap in the tech world.

Conversations with Women CEO's & Leaders

My Conversation With

Paige Arnof-Fenn
Founder & CEO Mavens & Moguls

I started a global marketing firm 14 years ago and have a staff of 45 contractors. After a corporate career followed by working for 3 startups and now 14 years of running my business here is what I have learned and helped build my confidence as an entrepreneur and business owner:

1) Jobs and job leads can come from anyone anywhere anytime so you should always be on your best behavior & make a great lasting impression. You'd be amazed where some of my best contacts have come from over the years a gardener who also happened to work for someone who was in a position to help, a hair stylist who had well heeled (and coiffed) clients, standing in line for the bathroom at a conference I struck up a conversation with a top recruiter. Seriously be nice to everyone & make friends before you need them, you never know who is in or will be in a position to help!

2) My biggest work regret is not getting rid of weak people earlier than I did in the first few years of my business. I knew in my gut they were not up to snuff but out of loyalty to them I let

them hang around much longer than they should have. It would have been better for everyone to let them go as soon as the signs were there. They became more insecure and threatened as we grew which was not productive for the team. As soon as I let them go the culture got stronger and the bar higher. "A" team people like to be surrounded by other stars. It is true that you should hire slowly and fire quickly. I did not make that mistake again later on so learned it well the first time. Lesson learned!

3) Marry the right person for the right reasons! I believe that much of your happiness and sadness in life comes from that single decision of choosing the right life partner.

4) People tell you to "never burn a bridge" but I can say that really is great advice and can tell you dozens of stories over the years where that has served me well. You just never know when your paths will cross again with old colleagues, former bosses, etc. I got an introduction to one of my best clients ever from an old friend who basically stole my idea for an article. I wanted to bust the friend for plagiarism but ended up taking the high road

instead and years later was remembered a someone who has great ideas which lead to the introduction to my client. Another time my boss' boss used to make my life miserable and after I left the company and got a much bigger job my former senior management tracked me to down to help get him into my new company when I was in a position to help which I did and now that we have both moved on from that firm he has become one of my biggest champions and references and now remembers me as a strong team player he discovered with loads of potential (versus the junior person who used to threaten him). Recently I pitched a new client who did not hire us and instead of being nasty about it I took the high road and she thought I handled defeat in such a classy way she has steered other business our way and wants to hire us for the next project. Kill them with kindness and don't ever burn that bridge, trust me it pays off!

5) Treat yourself as well as you'd treat your best client, you are not good to anyone else if you are not at your best so take good care, eat well, sleep, exercise, etc.

6) Instead of meeting up with your local friends at a coffee shop, a bar, over a meal or chatting with them on the phone, meet them for a bike ride or a walk so you can catch up while you are getting some exercise too. You'll feel great after, the time will fly & it will be a fun activity to share. It works professionally too, I have clients who play golf so sometimes we meet at a driving range instead of the office to discuss things especially when you are trying to think outside the box. A change in venue is always nice and you feel so much better when you are moving and not trapped behind your desk. Find creative ways to multi task that incorporates exercise & you'll be amazed how much more energy and time you have!

Conversations with Women CEO's & Leaders

My Conversation With
Maria Ioia
Founder and CEO of Market Intelligence Agency

Finding my confidence factor

I am Maria Ioia, author, founder and CEO of Market Intelligence Agency. Previously, I established the Competitive Intelligence function of the Commonwealth Bank of Australia (CBA). In 2014 I was awarded the *Women Leaders in Business award (UNSW Business School), Young entrepreneur of the year* and nominated for *Telstra Business Women's Award*.

I wasn't born with confidence, I was a shy, obedient child. I respected authority into my 20's and always worked my best, driven more from fear of failure than anything else. I placed incredible stress on myself in the process. This all changed when I was selected for an early leadership program whilst commencing studies for an Executive MBA and afforded the opportunity to provide regular updates to the board of CBA. This experience helped to build my confidence to back myself.

The biggest test in my confidence was in starting my own company. I continued to step up and be noticed although the stakes were higher. To deal with the anxiety in taking large risks, I had to learn about vulnerability. Knowing my purpose allowed me to stick with my chosen path regardless. This helped me to develop a strong opinion and express it with conviction.

Confidence in leadership is a journey of self-discovery allowing me to be the expert that I am. It is not easily rattled. To women who lack the belief in themselves as leaders, I challenge you. Step out from the safety of someone else's work or opinion. Challenge every insecurity you have and make peace with them. Only then can you take a deep breath and speak from deep within you. You already have the answers, and once you trust in that, there will be no turning back. Knowing yourself from within, is a powerful force to be reckoned with.

My Conversation With
Marne Martin
CEO of Service Power Technologies, Plc

Confidence to be indelible comes from within and while it may be bolstered by external validation, it must come from strong roots and an internal steadiness to take advantage of opportunities and challenges. The value of confidence is to be willing, with a minimum of drama, to meet challenges head on. Many think of confidence as an embodiment of extroversion, ego, or even as a representation of narcissism, but confidence is not linked to personality type. It is a belief in one's ability to take on challenges and persevere through hardship. While the expression of confidence may vary by personality, the belief one has or doesn't have it is something deeply seated inside. There are some people that have a fundamental drive to take risks and try new things. I likely had that as an advantage given that my first sentence was apparently "me can do it."

However, even though that may have indicated that an early "seed of confidence" was planted, it still had to be nurtured to grow into a sapling and then a strong and tall tree. It is normal for confidence to ebb and flow; however, each of us must watch our words and thoughts such that we are affirming our actions and learning from our failures, building rather than breaking down confidence. Even those that are confident in one area may not feel confident in others, but the way to become a confident person overall is to have belief that if a challenge presents itself, one will get through to the other side, whether work, personal, health, etc.

One of the greatest responsibilities parents and teachers therefore have is developing within girls and young women the self-confidence that not only withstand the tests of the schoolyards, but also prepares them to enter the working world. Confidence continues to grow, much like the mighty Redwoods in California or trees in the Amazon, but it has to begin from a seed, and that seed is usually laid in the early years of childhood.

Being successful in school, a sport, or a club activity will help girls find confidence among their peers, especially if that confidence comes from both knowing that they have a talent for something, but that they also become more successful at it with hard work. Those girls that only find confidence from things that come easily, usually have a harder time sustaining confidence in the face of the challenges that come with more sustained drive for career growth. In many cases, risk comes with reward, and one's confidence grows not only through successes but also withstanding and overcoming failures.

Those already in the working world that don't feel confident in their roles should clearly display confidence, and listen and collaborate with those around. Outside of work also be sure to find something easy at which you can be a success, "recharging" the confidence battery. And when something is difficult, buckle down and think of solutions. Don't focus on 'I can't'. Be a problem solver who 'can' overcome challenges in the workplace and create from them achievements. Withstand conflict and strife. Solve problems. All of these build confidence in the work environment.

In my late twenties, when I was first put in charge of operational management, it was a great achievement. At the age of 40, being appointed CEO of a public company was also a milestone. I was already a pretty confident person, but the ability to gain confidence not just leading people but actually managing and executing on business deliverables created a new facet of confidence. These business successes were born both of the confidence that I had the skills to persevere and earn respect, and that I fundamentally "had what it takes" even if there are always areas where one works to improve or be more effective.

Business is both challenging and very competitive. There is no other way for it to be, so being confident to wake up each day and know that the day's challenges are not too much to bear is critical. I am proud of many things in my life. Being a public company CEO is one of them as hopefully that inspires other girls to not only dream but to make it happen. However, I also take pride that as my sense of self-confidence evolved and grew better-rounded, I have worked to listen more and actually work with those around me to see what might be a seed or sapling, become for them to a tree. In an ideal world, confidence is shared and together we grow a forest.

A Conversation With
(Myself)
Carol Sankar
Founder of RRC, Inc.

I was in a place of resisting complacency when the market collapsed in 2009. The bottom literally fell for everyone and I watched the world in panic during one of the worst economic crises of my generation.

I remember getting dressed to run to Target to get a few supplies for the house one Friday afternoon when my husband called me frantically and told me to run and fill up my car with gas and get an oil change quickly. Ten minutes earlier, a price spike was announced that was about to make the cost of a gallon of petroleum over $5 per gallon at the station. I ran to the nearest gas station and sat in line with everyone else in a panic. Several stations literally closing after running out of gas for the day and the spike was not coming to an end any time soon.

2009 felt like Armageddon, the world was coming to an end unless we decided who was going to fix it. Banks were not lending, my bank closed my account due to cutbacks and lack of treasury bonds to back my cash. The price of milk and bread were soaring. I never witnessed this before.

I have lived through other recessions, but this one seemed too real for me. As a real estate investor, I wanted the bleeding to end. I could not buy or sell, I just sat. I started thinking about plan b as everyone around me started to sell me fear that the world would never get any better. The same year, I had this crazy idea to walk into the commercial real estate market and take a gamble while the market was collapsing. A wise man once told me that you have to run INTO what everyone else is running away FROM in order to find what they cannot see. I started looking at properties in Tennessee, Florida, Ohio, etc. I started to see prices at nearly 50% discount from where they were only 18 months prior. I knew I needed to find a way to make it happen.

Money was completely dried up, lenders could not lend. As a matter of fact, there are lenders who I used to do business offering to sell properties for pennies on the dollar. Then, one morning, out of the blue, I received a call from a broker in Atlanta, GA who was a trusted advisor of mine in the past. He had a 300 unit apartment complex with a shopping center attached to the property. My fear started to kick into overdrive as

I start thinking about funding a $2M property without a bank guarantee. People around me are selling me a mountain of fear, but I took a risk, and went to view it anyway.

It was truly abandoned and needed work, but I closed my eyes and saw the completed vision in my mind of how I can improve the property. It is rare that I fall in love with a project, but recognized the potential, while others recognized the problems. While on the site inspection, I called a funding agent and asked him to pull some strings for me, and within 24 hours, I had a financial commitment from a lending institution for $1.5 M. I negotiated the property down to $1.7M and we made a deal.

That is not even the end of the story, it is only the beginning. I made a huge leap for a woman who was accustomed to only negotiating under $150,000. I never thought in my lifetime that it would be a reality for me. However, I had to believe that I was running into the opportunity while the world was being sold scarcity and fear. I found loopholes and investors where others were becoming ultra conservative with their investments. The lesson: Be confident enough to recognize opportunities when others are running due to fear. The success you recognizing how to identify opportunities increases your confidence.

Conversations with Women CEO's & Leaders

My Conversation With
Hedy Popson
President of Productions Plus - The Talent Shop

You might look at my qualifications and assume I've never had confidence issues to overcome. As a young woman, I worked as an actress and spokesperson, appearing in over 100 television commercials and films. I've performed for audiences of over 5,000 people. I held the title of Miss Teen North America, spent time as a pageant and life coach and counseled executives from Fortune 100 companies. And today, with over 25 years of experience in the entertainment and automotive industries, I lead a national talent agency that specializes in providing auto show models to the top automakers on the globe.

But for a female business leader in the male-dominated automotive industry, it was initially hard to feel confident, even with a resume like mine. For me, finding my "Confidence Factor" has been a process rather than a watershed "A-ha!" moment.

To succeed in an environment entrenched in male leadership culture, I had to first recognize that my voice was needed; that my opinions mattered. I had to blur the lines between professional and personal confidence: I had to not only recognize and value my power in the workplace, but I had to live it all the time - at work, at home and in my relationships. Another "secret" to my success has come from learning how to take the emotion out of business while still operating with a level of empathy and understanding. Over time, I was able to turn into myself, trust my intuition and then follow it.

I don't believe women necessarily need to overcome anything to lead, but rather embrace our natural leadership attributes and believe in ourselves and then imbue those qualities into making work decisions and running our businesses. I have found that kind of "organically-grown" confidence and success go hand-in-hand.

Conversations with Women CEO's & Leaders

Conversations with Women CEO's & Leaders

My Conversation With
Eileen McDonnell
CEO of Penn Mutual Life Insurance Company

As the first female chief executive officer of 164-year-old Penn Mutual Life Insurance Company (www.pennmutual.com) and the first woman to lead any major life insurance company, I hold one of the coveted executive seats. I pursued a career in financial services with my eyes wide open but I never focused on the challenges of being an ambitious woman amid a male-dominated business nor did I try to fit in with the boys. To be successful, you first have to be authentic to yourself. From the beginning of my career, I made choices that put me in control of my own destiny including my work and personal life.

I graduated from Molloy College with a degree in mathematics and computer science then earned an MBA in finance and investments at Adelphi University. I spent a brief time at the now defunct Wang Laboratories then moved to AXA/Equitable. It was at Guardian Life Insurance Company where I began to hone in on life insurance and very quickly advance my career. By 27, I was a vice president.

By the time I was promoted to senior vice president at Guardian, my responsibilities expanded considerably. I directed strategic planning for the company's individual insurance products and managed the distribution network of 3,000 agents. During this time, my father became gravely ill. Shrewd financial planning allowed me to quit my job to take care of him. I used the cash value of a whole life insurance policy and savings to fund my absence from work.

A week after my father died, MetLife made me president of its subsidiary, New England Financial, within six months. Somewhere during that same period, I made the decision to adopt. I didn't have a biological child and had been privileged to enjoy the love of my own big extended family. I wanted to share that love with a child of my own.

The adoption process would require time away from my job. And, I knew that once I had my daughter, I'd want to take off from work so that we could get to know each other. Once again, I left my job and tapped my insurance and savings to pay for the choices I made. During her time away from the corporate world, I formed my own consulting business and taught at The American College so that I'd still be connected should I want to return to the insurance business.

Now as president and CEO of Penn Mutual and a member of its Board of Trustees, I am in charge of one of the biggest life insurance companies in the country. I manage every aspect of day-to-day operations for the company that provides life insurance and annuities. I am a chairman of the Board of Hornor Townsend & Kent, serve on the Board of Managers of Janney Montgomery Scott LLC and on the Pennsylvania Trust Company Board of Directors, all wholly-owned subsidiaries of Penn Mutual.

I also serve on the board of directors of LL Global, Inc., the holding company for LIMRA and LOMA, two of the world's largest insurance and financial services trade organizations. Additionally, I am a national advisor to Vision 2020, a national project of Drexel University College of Medicine Institute for Women's Health and Leadership. Vision 2020 is focused on advancing gender equality by energizing the dialogue about women and leadership.

In spite of the many duties of a demanding career, I have managed to strike a balance between work and home life. I believe Penn Mutual's company culture has been central in my ability to do so. I also credit my family for providing the kind of support structure to allow me to have both career and child. It's also about choice. I could have hired a live-in nanny but knew that childcare arrangement wouldn't make me happy. Instead made the decision to move my mother, sister and my family from Long Island to the Philadelphia area.

With extended family around, we enjoy life together, especially outdoors. I believe a child's play is their work, so I try to spend time having fun with her.

My career didn't happen to me, I made it happen. Although it's impossible to anticipate all of the changes that life brings, I know that planning for all of life's possibilities, assures that you can face whatever comes your way with some measure of confidence.

Conversations with Women CEO's & Leaders

My Conversation With
Lori Florio & Emily Vitale
Founders of PRISMSPORT

"In terms of confidence, this was developed over time through every person who believed in us and the ones who assisted in our next steps," Lori Florio and Emily Vitale said.

It's the bottom of the mountain analogy- when you look to the top, it's difficult, but when you're just looking to next step, you see that it's feasible. It's about keeping that mindset at all times.

"I wouldn't say I'm a super confident person, however, I've learned through the years that confidence comes from handling the small parts of projects rather than worrying about the whole project," Vitale said, "Anne Lamott's book, *Bird by Bird* has many passages that resonate with me, especially the concept of taking a project and working it through it step by step."

In addition, both women tend stand back and observe first. Their brains need to work through a concept in its entirety before delving right in.

"I recently started taking Parkour Classes and before I could commit, I had to go and watch, absorb before I could sign up!" Vitale said. Florio and I have a phrase, "thoughts in the night," which translates to, our best ideas come up often without forcing ourselves and worrying.

The earliest obstacle that Florio and Vitale confronted in starting PRISMSPORT was determining whether or not they had a viable concept in marrying fashion and true performance.

"We always had confidence in our vision and our fashion sense," Florio said, "we also understood sports and knew that we had the expertise to make a performance garment."

Having not done this before and starting from scratch with a concept was an obstacle in itself. However, they weren't going to know if their concept would work, without taking on the basics of manufacturing a garment. One of the most exciting moments and confidence boosters for them was (after months of figuring out where to buy fabric, testing patterns, creating a logo, and finding a manufacturer), finally seeing their first garment sewn, tagged, and bagged!

This first huge step was an acknowledgment that they didn't need to know everything to get to where they were going.

"It didn't take long to find that we did (and do) have a viable concept," Florio said, "we focused first on our friends and dedicated athletes, especially spinners and yogi's, who reinforced the viability and authenticity of our brand. They loved our pants and helped us spread the word."

The majority of obstacles were overcome by learning as much as they could through talking with other people, the internet and researching everything they could get their hands on that was relative.

"Most of what got us over the variety of humps were the friends that we made and the people willing to help out and give advice (both in and outside the industry)," Florio and Vitale said.

Soon, retail stores asked to carry the line. Once they started selling at direct to consumer events and saw the great response, that turned into wholesale. A big confidence booster was getting an unsolicited phone call from Anthropologie, asking to come and see the line! Immediately after was Bloomingdales, who contacted through the PRISMSPORT website, asking if they were interested in being a retailer.

"Those were the moments for us when we thought, oh my gosh, we might have made it," Florio and Vitale said.

Now our challenge is dealing with an overwhelming crowded marketplace; we need maintain our confidence that our product is different than the rest and resonates with our customers and prospective clientele.

These women spend a decent amount of time researching and doing their homework. There is always another person who started a fitness, another bigger name, new venture capital backing, etc.

"We have confidence that our product can compete against all of these, we just have to keep taking it day by day (one obstacle after the next) and not get ahead of ourselves," Vitale said, "we have a show this weekend, we have a line to develop that we know well how to do..."

"We know how to do the work to get where we're going, we don't want to lose track of that with all of the distractions in the marketplace," Florio said.

"Maintaining our vision, positivity and our confidence, is what keeps us going every single day," Flori and Vitale said.

Acknowledgements

I would personally like to thank all of the leaders in this installment of the Confidence Factor for Women in Leadership. Every woman in this book brings a unique leadership style and quality that every reader can relate to. As I said earlier, these are the conversations I wish I had in the early stages of building my first company over a decade ago. Women who are seeking to accelerate their success and elevate past the infancy stage of building a business need to connect and converse with successful women. Success requires new posture and a new inner circle. I am honored to consider these women in leadership as a part of my inner circle and humbled by their transparency.

Thank you!

About Carol Sankar

Carol Sankar is a business advisor for high level, service based visionaries and executives, as well as leadership expert who is committed to assisting passionate leaders simplify their lives while increasing revenue by becoming productive, not working harder.

 She has been featured in numerous magazines, radio shows, articles and conferences; including a recent features in Madame Noire, Entrepreneur.com, TEDx, The Steve Harvey Show, CNNMoney.com, Daily Worth and Essence Magazine.

For more information about The Confidence Factor for Women in Leadership Round-table discussions, visit http://www.theconfidencefactorforwomen.com. We are an incubator for women with proven wisdom, experience, business & academic acumen, which is required for the level of coterie.

www.ingramcontent.com/pod-product-compliance
Lightning Source LLC
Chambersburg PA
CBHW070156100426
42743CB00013B/2931